SEASONAL CHORALE PRELUI
(WITH PEDALS)

Edited by C. H. TREVOR

BOOK II

NOTE

Although some of the pieces in this collection are suitable for particular seasons of the Church's year, they can be used for recitals and voluntaries at any time.

The tempo indications and registration are the editor's. They are merely suggestions and should be regarded as such.

The directions for registration which are enclosed in brackets may be used or not at the player's discretion.

Stops with the same names do not always produce the same effect on different organs. Players should use other registrations if those suggested are not effective or suitable on any particular instrument.

Where a note has a dot thus $\dot{\rho}$, it indicates either (a) the repetition of a note or (b) the end of a phrase.

In order to make clear the movement of the parts in some pieces, certain notes should be tied as indicated by the dotted lines thus .·˙˙·.

All the pieces in both books can be played effectively on an organ of two manuals and pedals. Most of them can be played on an instrument of one manual and pedals.

Where the registration is given for a small organ, it can be modified at the discretion of the player who has at his disposal an instrument of greater resources.

A number of short chorale preludes have been included, as pieces of this length are sometimes required.   *C.H.T.*

Book I consists of pieces for Advent, Christmas, Epiphany,
Lent, Passiontide, and general use.

*The illustration on the front cover is
of King's College Chapel, Cambridge.*

OXFORD UNIVERSITY PRESS
MUSIC DEPARTMENT · 44 CONDUIT STREET · LONDON W.1

ALPHABETICAL INDEX
BOOKS I and II

SEASONAL INDEX

BOOK II

SEASONAL CHORALE PRELUDES

(WITH PEDALS)

Edited by C. H. TREVOR

Book II

ERSCHIENEN IST DER HERRLICHE TAG

(Easter)

H. von Herzogenberg (1843-1900)

This melody is sung to the words (a) "Our Lord is risen from the dead"
(b) "Light's glittering morn bedecks the sky."

Printed in Great Britain
OXFORD UNIVERSITY PRESS, MUSIC DEPARTMENT, 44 CONDUIT STREET, LONDON W.1

Seasonal Chorale Preludes (Book II) with Pedals

4

ERSCHIENEN IST DER HERRLICHE TAG

(Easter)

Gt. & Sw. Diapasons 8. 4. 2. Mixture(s).
Ped. 16. 8. 4. Reed(s) 16. (8.) [or Reeds 16. 8. alone.]
Sw. to Gt.
Gt. & Sw. to Ped.

J. G. Walther (1684-1748)

Molto maestoso e marcato

Alternative registrations:

Gt. Diapasons 8. 4. (2.)	Gt. Diapasons 8. 4. 2.
Sw. Diapasons 8. 4. 2. (Mixture.)	Sw. Reed(s).
Ped. 16. 8.	Ped. 16. 8.
Sw. to Gt.	Gt. & Sw. to Ped.
Gt. & Sw. to Ped.	

This melody is sung to the words (a) "Our Lord is risen from the dead"
(b) "Light's glittering morn bedecks the sky."

allargando

Seasonal Chorale Preludes (Book II) with Pedals

6

MACHE DICH, MEIN GEIST, BEREIT
(Easter)

Gt. Diapasons 8. 4. (2.)
Sw. Diapasons 8. 4. 2. (Mixture.)
Ped. 16. 8.
Sw. to Gt.
Gt. & Sw. to Ped.

J. C. Kittel (1732-1809)
pupil of J. S. Bach

This melody is sung to the words "Christ the Lord is risen again."

CHRIST IST ERSTANDEN

(Easter)

The pedal part should be independent e.g. 16. 8. 4. uncoupled. If this is not possible, 16. 8.
can be coupled to appropriate stops on a manual not in use.

R.H. { Gt. Trumpet (or Diapason) 8. (Principal 4.) }
{ (Fifteenth 2.) Mixture. }
L.H.   Sw. Diapasons 8. 4. 2. Mixture.
Ped. 16. 8. 4.
(Sw. to Gt.)
Sw. to Ped.

J. Buchner (1483-1538)

Alternative registrations:
R.H. Gt. Diapason(s) 8. (4.)   R.H. Sw. Trumpet 8. Principal 4. Fifteenth 2. Mixture.
L.H. Sw. Diapasons 8. 4. (2.)   L.H. Gt. Flutes 8. 4. (Fifteenth 2.)
Ped. 16. 8.   Ped. 16. 8.
(Sw. to Gt.)   Gt. to Ped.
Sw. to Ped.

This melody is sometimes sung to the words "Jesus lives! thy terrors now."

Seasonal Chorale Preludes (Book II) with Pedals

KOMM, GOTT SCHÖPFER, HEILIGER GEIST
(Whitsuntide)

Man. Ch. Flute 4.
Ped. coupled to Sw. Principal 4.
(Ch. to Ped.)

J. G. Walther (1684-1748)

Alternative registrations:

Man. Gt. Flute 4.	Man. Ch. Flutes 8. 4.	R.H. Gt. Flute 8.
Ped. coupled to Sw. Principal 4.	Ped. coupled to Sw. Oboe (or Diapason) 8. (Principal 4.) (Fifteenth 2.)	L.H. Ch. Flutes 8. 4.
(Gt. to Ped.)		Sw. soft reeds. 16. 8.
		Sw. to Ped.

This melody is sung to the words "Come, Holy Ghost, our souls inspire."

Seasonal Chorale Preludes (Book II) with Pedals

9

Seasonal Chorale Preludes (Book II) with Pedals

NUN BITTEN WIR DEN HEILGEN GEIST

(Whitsuntide)

R.H. Sw. Diapason 8.
L.H. Gt. soft 8. (or Ch. Flutes 8. 4.)
Ped. soft 16. (8.)
Gt. (or Ch.) to Ped.

The metronome rate is a suggestion as to speed. The crotchet pulse should be felt.

D. Buxtehude (1637-1707)

Adagio ma non troppo (♩ = about 88)

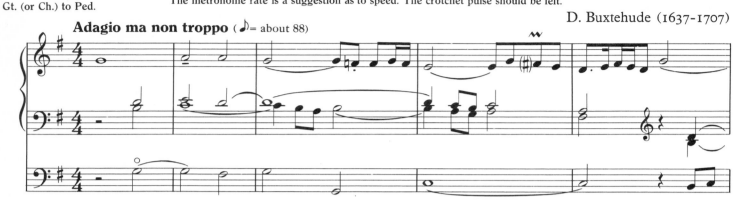

Alternative registrations:

R.H. Ch. Flutes 8. 4. Larigot 1⅓ (or Nazard 2⅔)	R.H. Gt. Dulciana (or Flute) 8.	R.H. Ch. Gamba (or Clarinet) 8. Flute 4.
L.H. Sw. soft 8. (or Flutes 8. 4.)	L.H. Sw. soft 8.	L.H. Sw. soft 8. (4.)
Ped. 16.	Ped. soft 16.	Ped. soft 16. (8.)
Sw. to Ped.	(Sw. to Gt.)	Sw. to Ped.
	Sw. to Ped.	

Seasonal Chorale Preludes (Book II) with Pedals

DER DU BIST DREI IN EINIGKEIT

(Trinity)

Gt. Diapason(s) 8. (4.) (2.)
Ped. 16. 8.
Gt. to Ped.

J. F. Alberti (1642–1710)

Andante maestoso (♩ = about 60)

Seasonal Chorale Preludes (Book II) with Pedals

VATER UNSER IM HIMMELREICH
(Trinity)

R.H. Sw. Diapason (or Oboe) 8.
L.H. Gt. soft 8. (or Ch. Flutes 8. 4.)
Ped. 16.
Gt. (or Ch.) to Ped.

J. Weinmann (died 1542)

NUN LASST UNS GOTT DEM HERREN

(Festivals or General)

Gt. Diapasons 8. 4. 2.
Sw. Diapasons 8. 4. 2. Reed 8. [or Reed(s) alone.]
Ped. 16. 8.
Gt. & Sw. to Ped.

F. W. Zachau (1663-1712)
teacher of Handel

Moderato ma con moto

Seasonal Chorale Preludes (Book II) with Pedals

Seasonal Chorale Preludes (Book II) with Pedals

LOBE DEN HERREN, DEN MÄCHTIGEN KÖNIG DER EHREN

(Festivals or General)

Gt. Diapasons 8. 4. (2.)
Sw. Diapasons 8. 4. 2. (Mixture.)
Ped. 16. 8.
Sw. to Gt.
Gt. & Sw. to Ped.

J. G. Walther (1684-1748)

Alternative registrations:
Gt. & Sw. Diapasons 8. 4. 2. Mixtures.
Ped. { (32.) 16. 8. 4. Reed(s) 16. (8.) }
{ or Reeds (32.) 16. 8. alone. }
Sw. to Gt.
Gt. & Sw. to Ped.

Gt. Diapasons 8. 4. 2. (Mixture.)
Sw. Reed(s) (16.) 8. (4.)
Ped. 16. 8.
Gt. & Sw. to Ped.

This melody is sung to the words "Praise to the Lord, the Almighty, the King of creation."

Seasonal Chorale Preludes (Book II) with Pedals

Seasonal Chorale Preludes (Book II) with Pedals

HERR GOTT, DICH LOBEN ALLE WIR

(Festivals or General)

Gt. (or Ch.) Flute 4. both hands.
Ped. coupled to Sw. Principal 4.
[Gt. (or Ch.) to Ped.]

This piece can effectively be played either loudly or softly.

J. Pachelbel (1653-1706)

Alternative registrations:
Gt. Diapasons 8. 4. 2.
Sw. Diapasons 8. 4. 2. Reed 8. [or Reed(s) alone.]
Ped. 16. 8.
Gt. & Sw. to Ped.

Gt. & Sw. Diapasons 8. 4. 2. Mixtures.
Ped. 16. 8. 4. Reeds 16. 8. [or Reed(s) 16. (8.) alone.]
Sw. to Gt.
Gt. & Sw. to Ped.

This melody is sung to the words "All people that on earth do dwell."

Seasonal Chorale Preludes (Book II) with Pedals

19

Seasonal Chorale Preludes (Book II) with Pedals

HERR GOTT, DICH LOBEN ALLE WIR

(Festivals or General)

Gt. Diapasons 8. 4. 2.
Sw. { Diapasons 8. 4. 2. Reed 8. }
{ or Reed(s) alone. }
Ped. 16. 8.
Gt. & Sw. to Ped.

G. F. Kauffmann (1679-1735)

Alternative registration:
Gt. & Sw. Diapasons 8. 4. 2. Mixtures.
Ped. { 32. 16. 8. 4. Reeds 16. 8. }
{ or Reeds 32. 16. 8. alone. }
Sw. to Gt.
Gt. & Sw. to Ped.

This melody is sung to the words "All people that on earth do dwell."

Seasonal Chorale Preludes (Book II) with Pedals

HERR GOTT, DICH LOBEN ALLE WIR
(Festivals or General)

Gt. & Sw. Diapasons 8. 4. 2.
Ped. 16. 8.
Sw. to Gt.
Gt. & Sw. to Ped.

G. Merkel (1827-1885)

This melody is sung to the words "All people that on earth do dwell."

Seasonal Chorale Preludes (Book II) with Pedals

NUN FREUT EUCH, LIEBEN CHRISTEN G'MEIN

(Festivals or General)

The manuals should be equally balanced but different in tone quality.

I Gt. Diapasons 8. 4. (2.)
II Sw. Diapasons 8. 4. 2. (Mixture.)
Ped. 16. 8. 4. Reed 16. [or Reed(s) 16. (8.) alone.]
Gt. & Sw. to Ped.

H. F. Quehl (18th century)

Allegro brillante (♩ = 72-80)

Alternative registration for a small organ: I Gt. Flutes 8. 4.
II Sw. Diapasons 8. 4. (2.)
Ped. 16. 8.
Gt. & Sw. to Ped.

Seasonal Chorale Preludes (Book II) with Pedals

Seasonal Chorale Preludes (Book II) with Pedals

MIR NACH, SPRICHT CHRISTUS UNSER HELD

(General)

Sw. soft 8.
Gt. soft 8. 4.
Gt. to Ped.

E. F. Wolf (died 1772)

Andante

This melody is sung to the words "O love, how deep! how broad! how high!"

Seasonal Chorale Preludes (Book II) with Pedals

WAS MEIN GOTT WILL, DAS G'SCHEH ALLZEIT

(General)

Gt. soft 8. (4.) [or Ch. Clarinet 8.]
Sw. soft 8. (or Flutes 8. 4.)
Ped. soft 16.
Sw. to Ped.

G. Merkel (1827-1885)

This melody is an adaptation of the old French folk-song, "Il me souffit des tous mes maulx."

Seasonal Chorale Preludes (Book II) with Pedals

IN DICH HAB ICH GEHOFFET, HERR
(General)

Ch. (or Sw.) Flutes 8. 4.
Ped. soft 16.
Ch. (or Sw.) to Ped.

J. C. Bach (1642-1703)
uncle of J. S. Bach

Alternative registration:
Sw. Diapason 8. [or soft 8ft. stop(s).]
Ped. soft 16.
Sw. to Ped.

Seasonal Chorale Preludes (Book II) with Pedals

DER HERR IST MEIN GETREUER HIRT

(General)

Gt. (or Sw.) Diapason 8.
Ped. 16. (8.)
Gt. (or Sw.) to Ped.

J. Pachelbel (1653-1706)

Seasonal Chorale Preludes (Book II) with Pedals

DIE HIMMEL RÜHMEN DES EWIGEN EHRE

(General)

Gt. Diapasons 8. 4. (2.)
Ped. 16. 8.
Gt. to Ped.

M. G. Fischer (1773-1829)

Allegro moderato

WACHET AUF, IHR FAULEN CHRISTEN

(General)

Gt. Diapasons 8. 4. 2.
Sw. Full without 16.ˢ
Ped. 16. 8.
Sw. to Gt.
Gt. & Sw. to Ped.

M. G. Fischer (1773-1829)

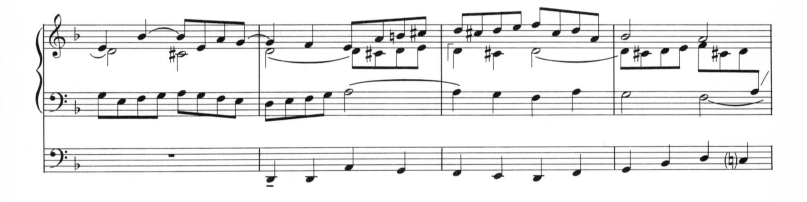

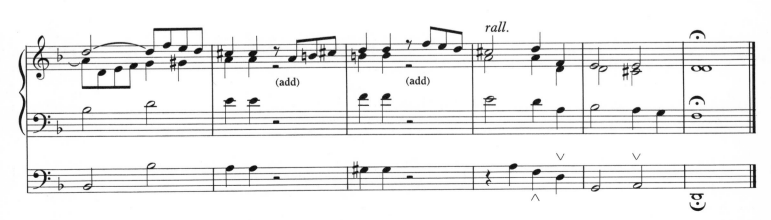

Seasonal Chorale Preludes (Book II) with Pedals

WER NUR DEN LIEBEN GOTT LÄSST WALTEN

(General)

Gt. (or Sw.) Diapasons 8.
Ped. 16. (8.)
Gt. (or Sw.) to Ped.

G. Merkel (1827-1885)

This melody is sung to the words "O Love, Who formedst me to wear."

Seasonal Chorale Preludes (Book II) with Pedals

Processed and printed by
Halstan & Co. Ltd., Amersham, Bucks., England